READY FOR A TWIST!

DEDICATION

This coloring book is dedicated first and foremost to the inner artist in YOU! I want to also dedicate these books to my daughter **Aija Kay Brown.** It's because of you I continue to work hard every day!

ACKNOWLEDGMENTS

The success of this book would not have been complete without the help from my close family and friends. Mom, Thanks for raising a great little person instilled with morals and hardworking work ethics.

Aunt Alicia and Uncle June, you have been there with me from the beginning, never telling me what I can't do, but always supporting me in the depths of it all.

A debt of gratitude is owed to My Uncle and God Father, world renowned Artist Ansel "Melvin" Butler. Thank you for telling it to me straight. For always pushing me to be better and to excel even MORE!

Lastly, but certainly not least Twisted Dips Art Studio staff, family and friends!!! You ALL rock! Thank you for lending a helping hand when needed at the studio! Jeb, CC, Mani, Mira, Eboski, Ni Ni, Krys and Nate, Kristen, and Duane.

NEVER SETTLE AND KEEP GOING!

Copyright © 2018 Kamille Brown

All rights reserved.

FROM THE ARTIST!

THANK YOU FOR YOUR SUPPORT WITH THE PURCHASE OF THIS BOOK! I'VE ALWAYS WANTED TO WRITE A BOOK, SO I DID! MY WORDS ARE THROUGH THE LINES IN EACH PAGE. THE LINES ARE MY WORDS THAT TELL EACH STORY! WHEN YOU COLOR, DOODLE, SCRIBBLE, OR WRITE IN THIS COLORING BOOK, YOU ARE READING AND HELPING WRITE THE STORY ALONG THE WAY. BECAUSE OF THIS, THROUGHOUT THE BOOK, <u>YOU WILL</u> SEE ORIGINAL COPIES OF THE HAND DRAWN PAGE. THERE ARE PLENTY OF WAYS TO COLOR OR FILL IN THE PAGES.

RELAX, ENJOY AND TRUST THE PROCESS. ART ISN'T ALWAYS INSTANT! THIS COLORING BOOK IS AN EXTENSION OF TWISTED DIPS ART STUDIO, WHERE ART IS YOUR WAY! LIKE NIKE SAYS, JUST DO IT! ITS JUST ART AND YOU CAN'T MESS UP! AFTER ALL IT'S YOUR WAY!!!

FROM MY PENS, MARKERS, CRAYONS AND MIXED MEDIAS

TO YOURS, HAPPY CREATING!

-KAM

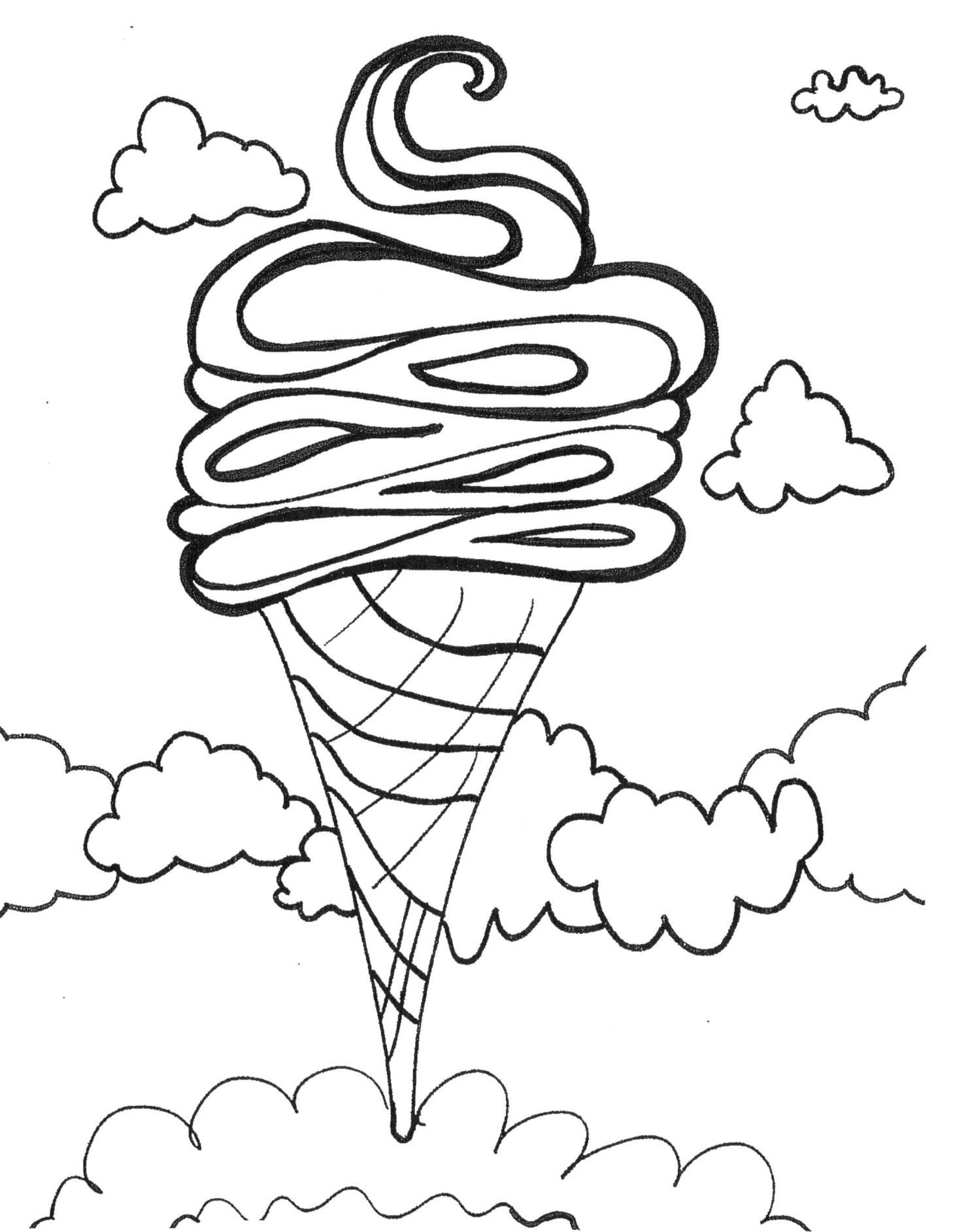

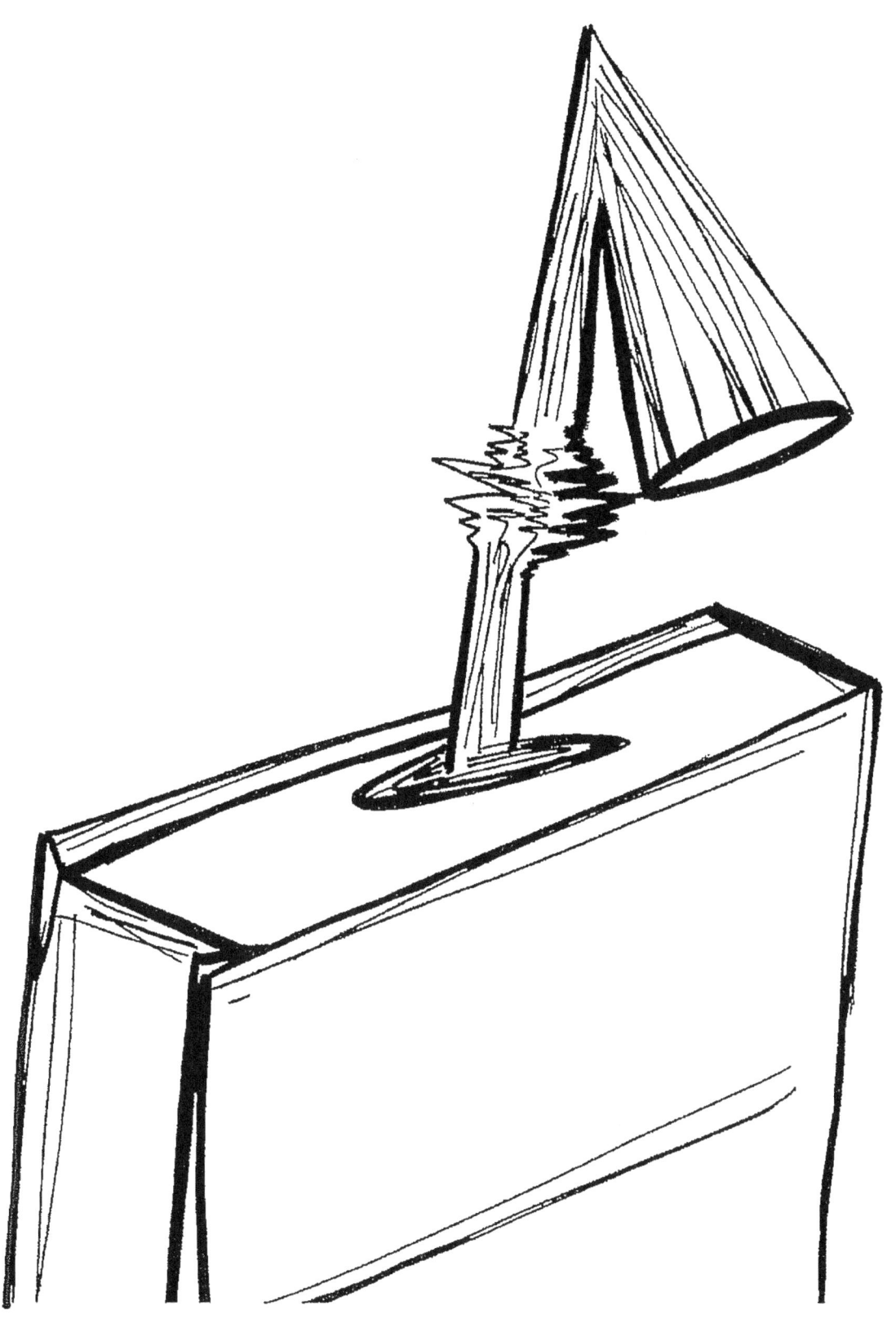

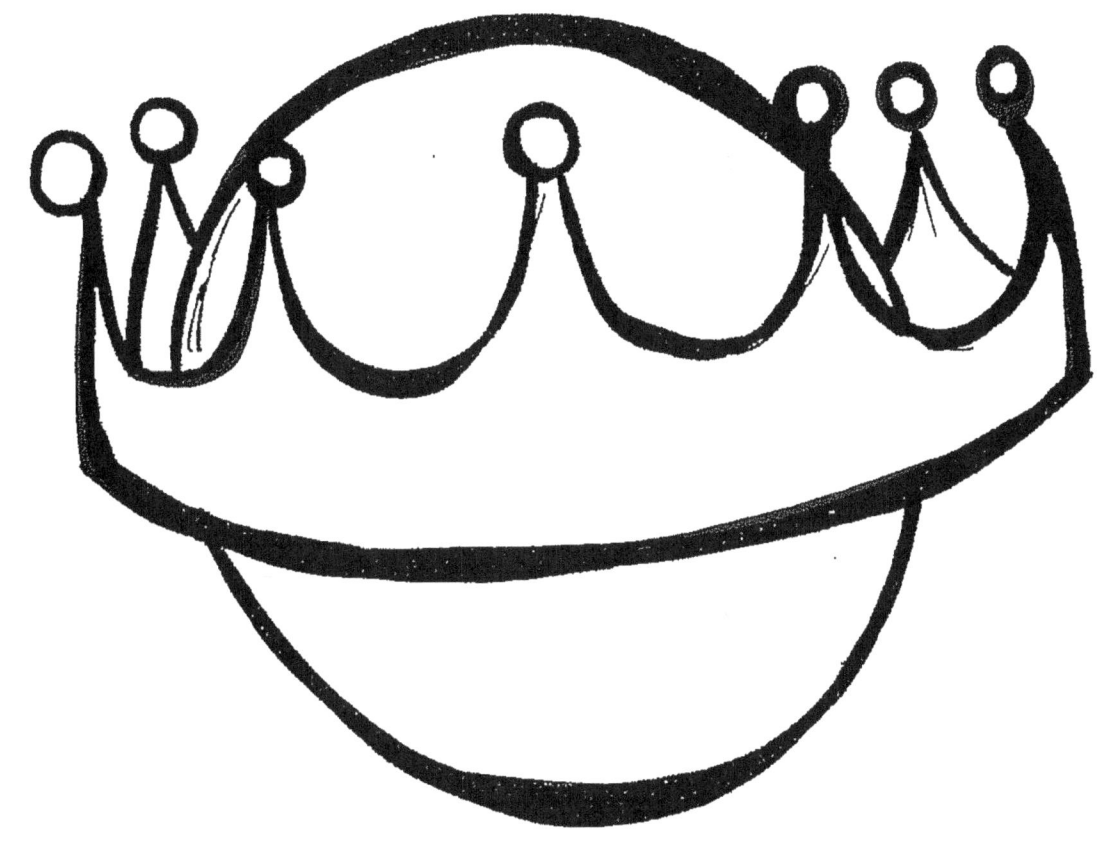

THE WORLD IS YOURS ! MAKE IT

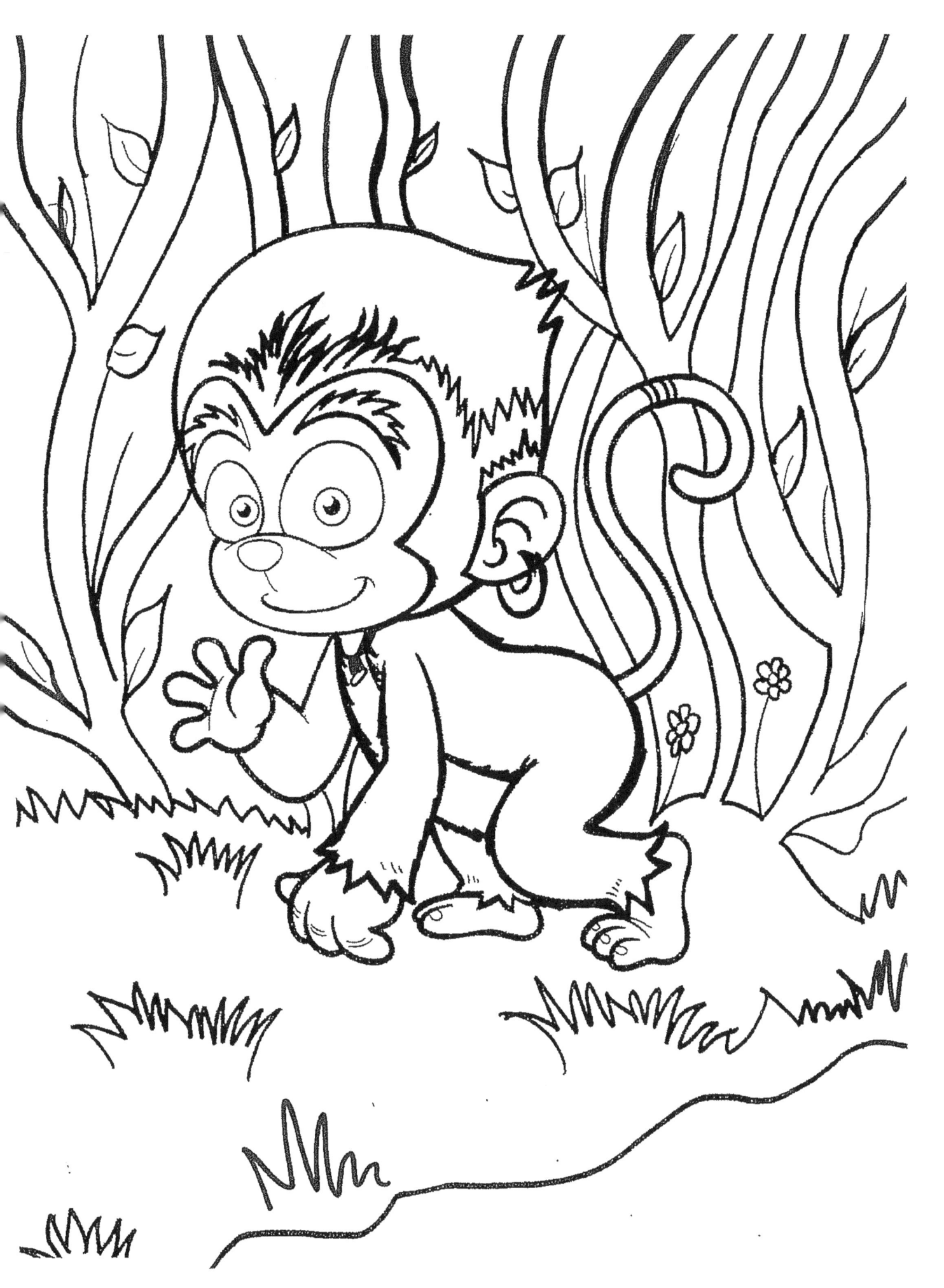

JUST CONNECT THE DOTS HERE!

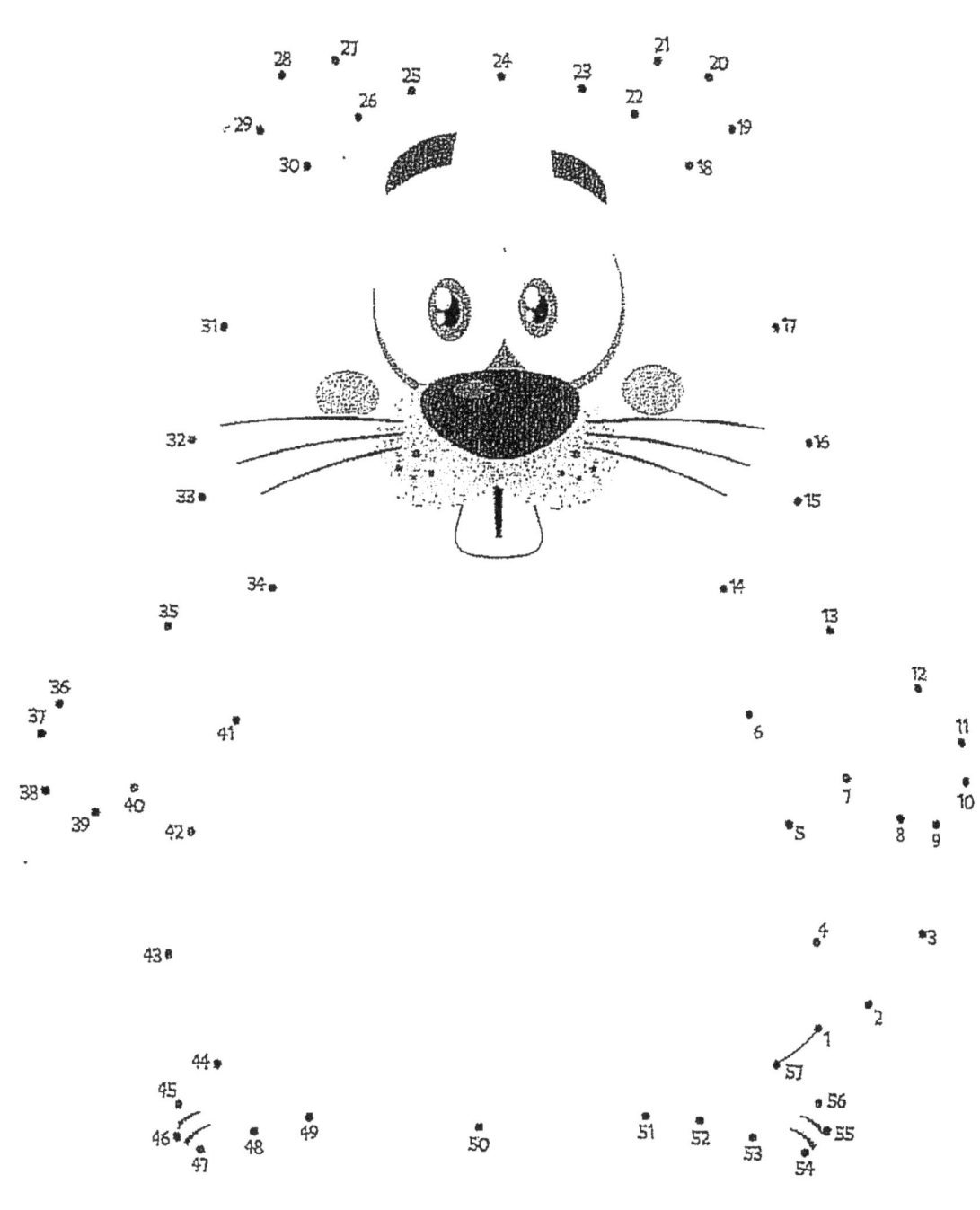

GUESS WHO?

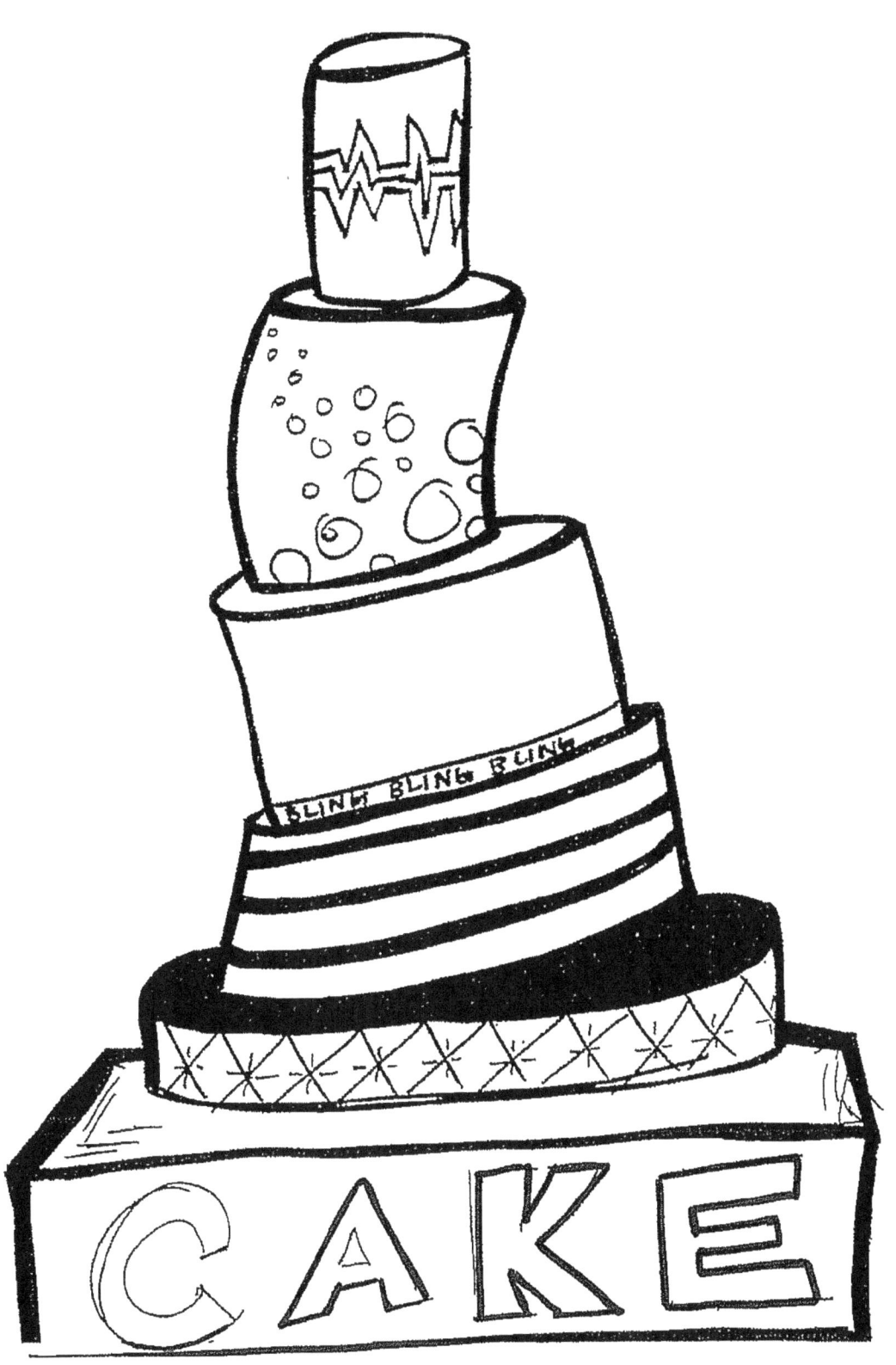

GRAB A HOMIE!!!
Tic Tac Toe

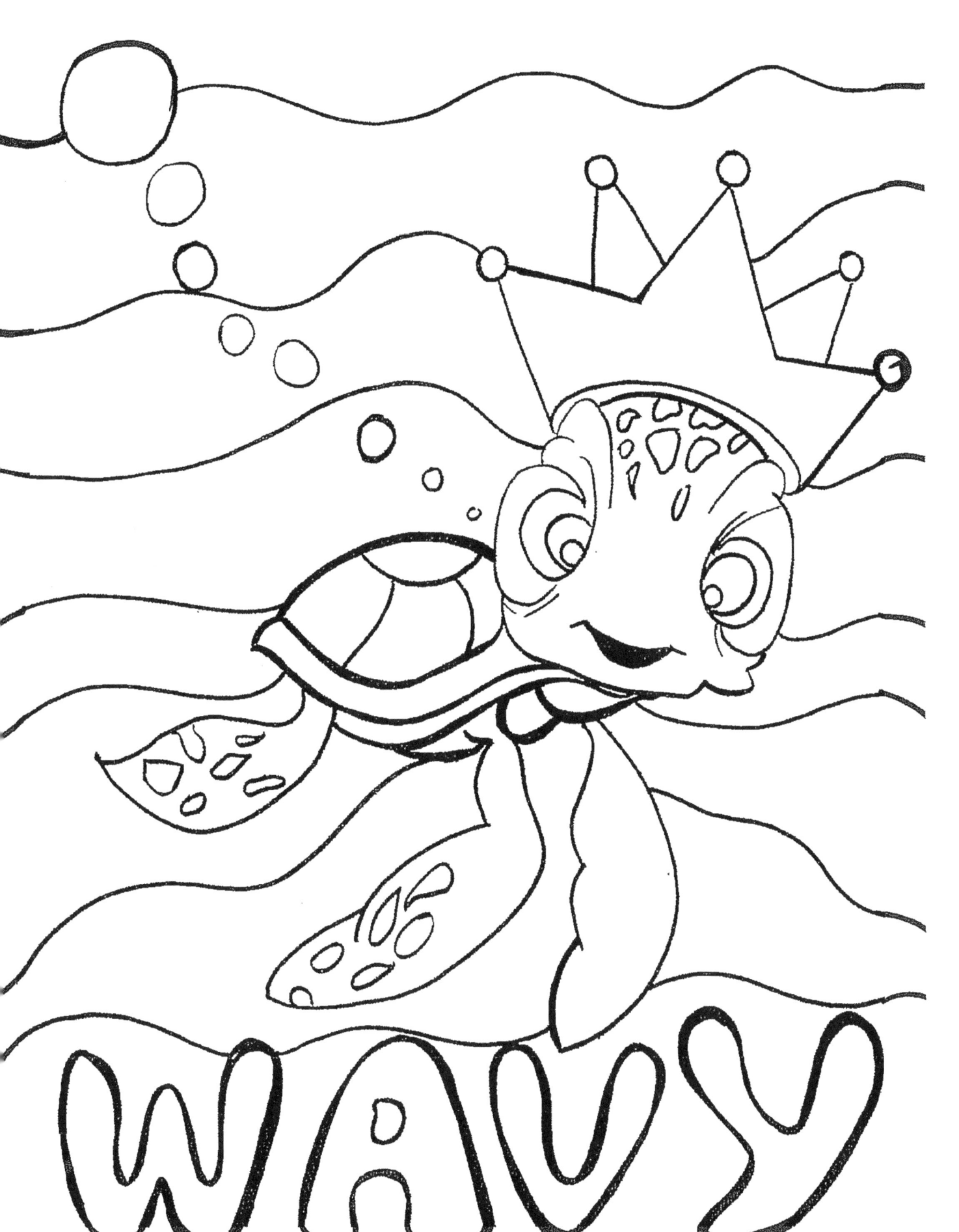

Twisted Dips Atl Kidz Art Search

```
C P L C R E A T E E U S S E A
P A M J X T Y O X I L V F C H
L I N I F Z Q D A I F E D O G
H N J V G G O Z C F E F U N X
Y T Y G A J D N A O I F B B Z
K W R O X S E V Q E O W I U J
L S S U A P T L B Z A U X L H
O J J P C V Y F G T N P F L O
C F M R H G R S E I V G X D R
Z K E E N N Y R E F O H H M E
D Q V D K J I B S H F O I I T
J H O V E K W H J E S V A T T
L X L L Q S O E P O T U I K I
T U S G R O L O C R I E R L L
O E L N B V G Z A L Q Q Z B G
```

ART	BRUSHES	CANVAS
COLOR	CREATE	FUN
GLITTER	LIFE	LOVE
PAINT	PENCILS	WATER

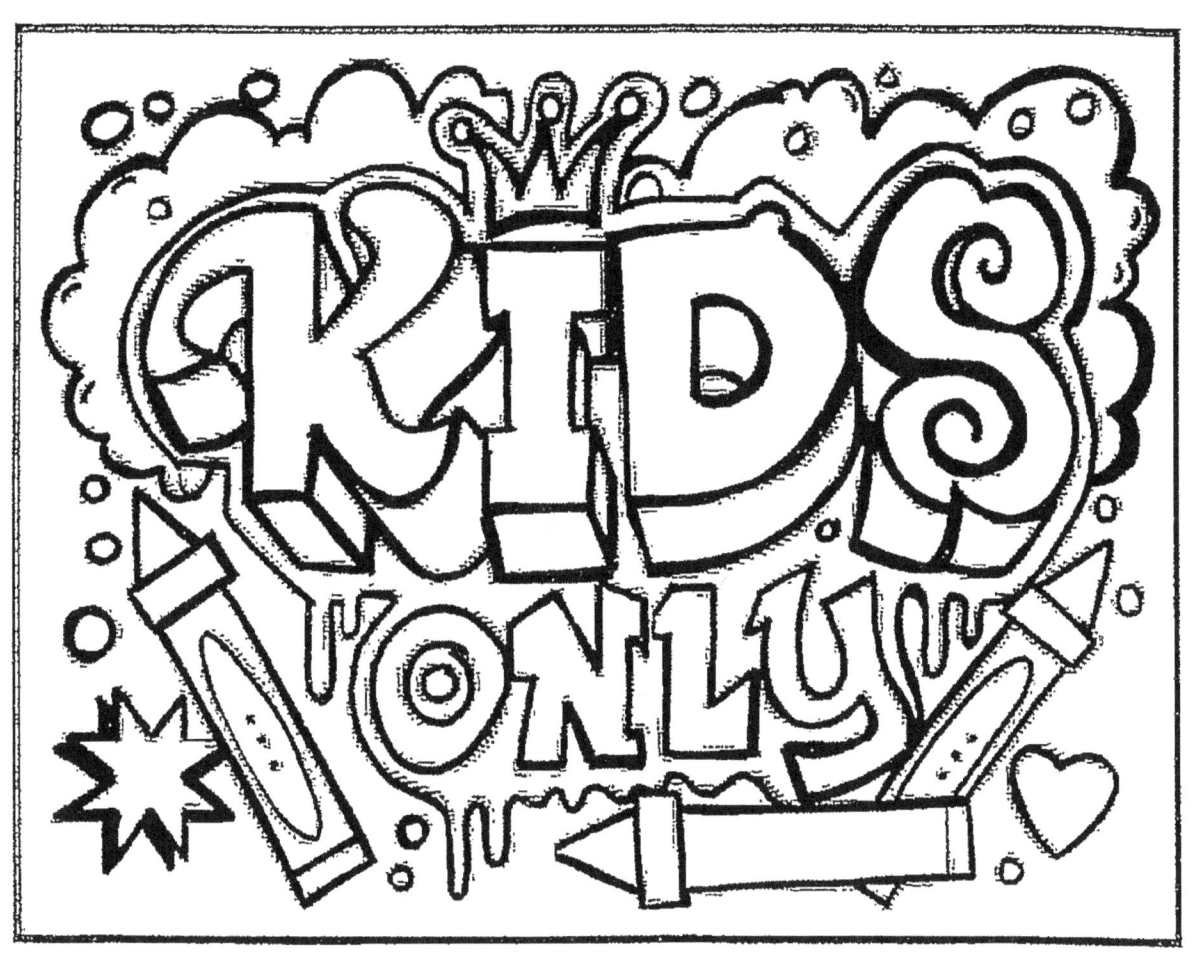

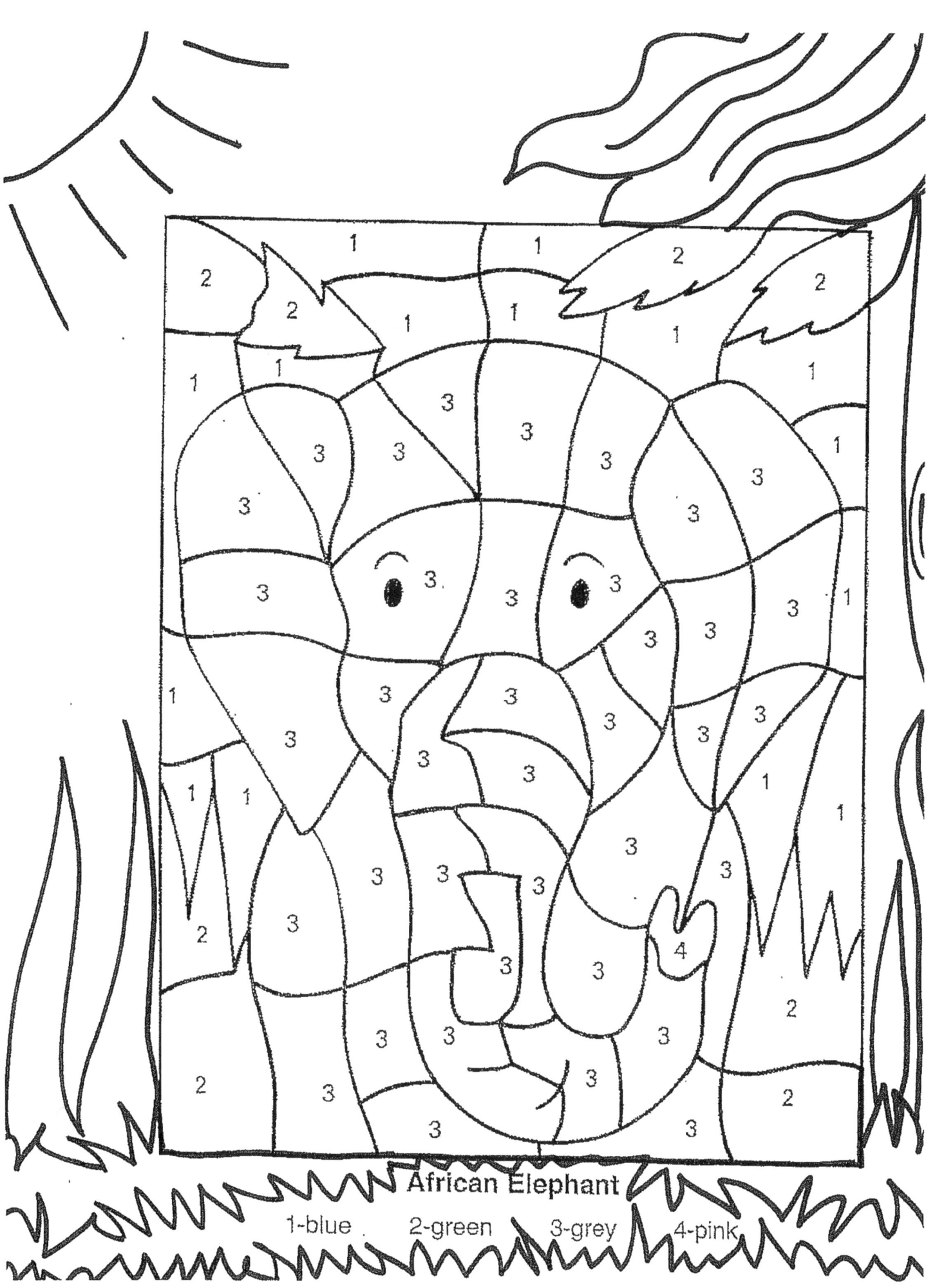

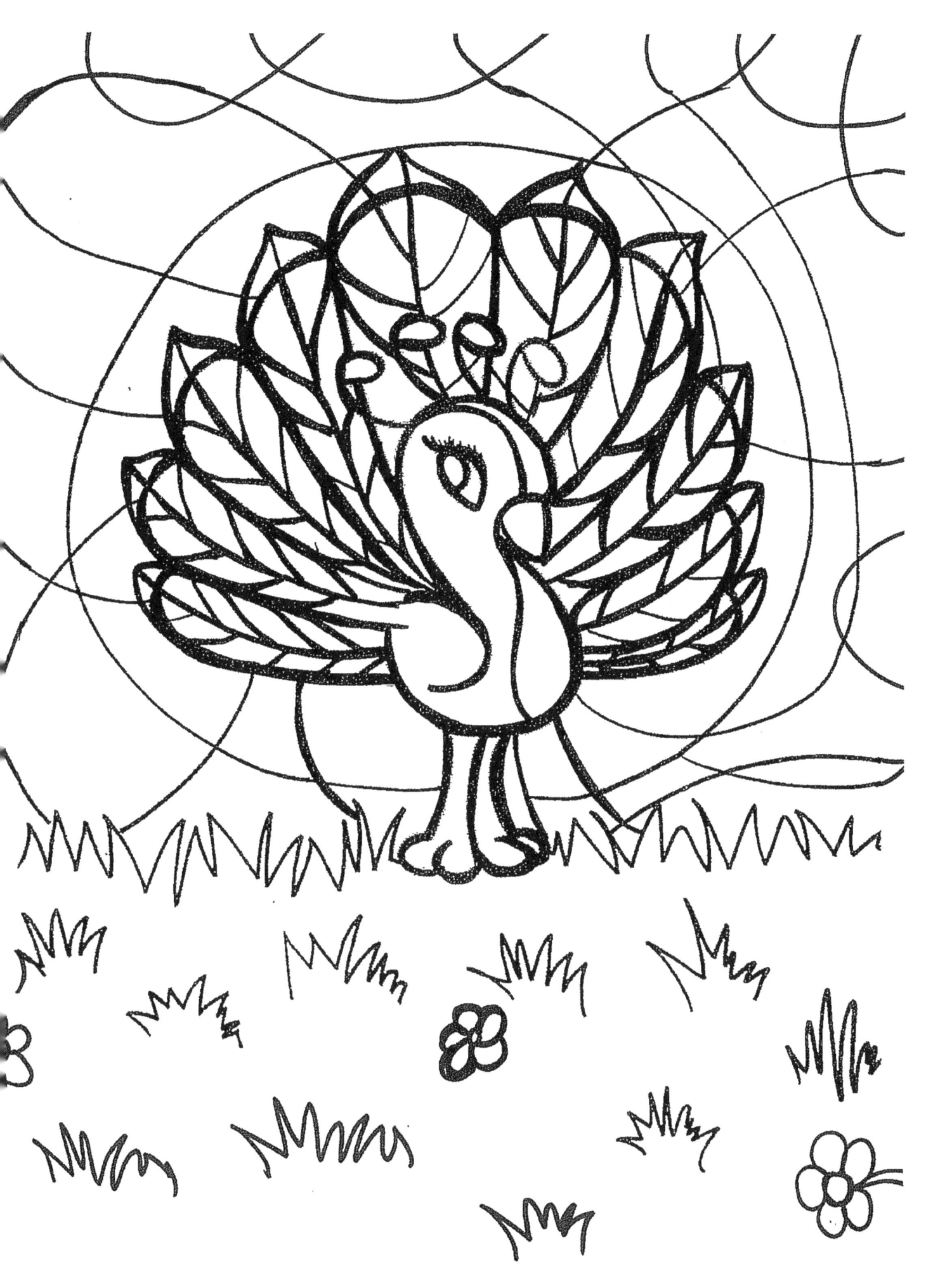

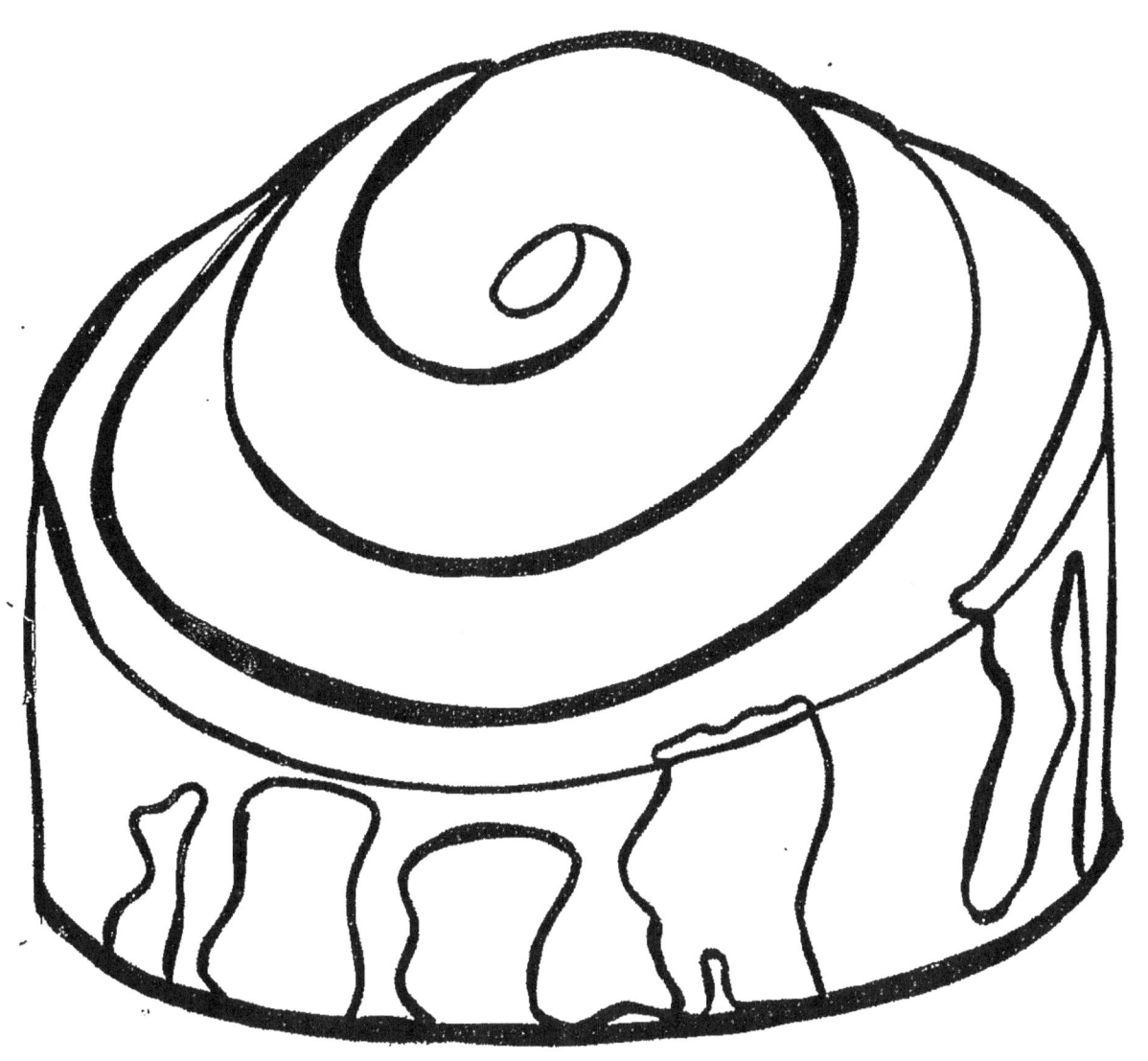

PICK YOUR OWN COLORS!

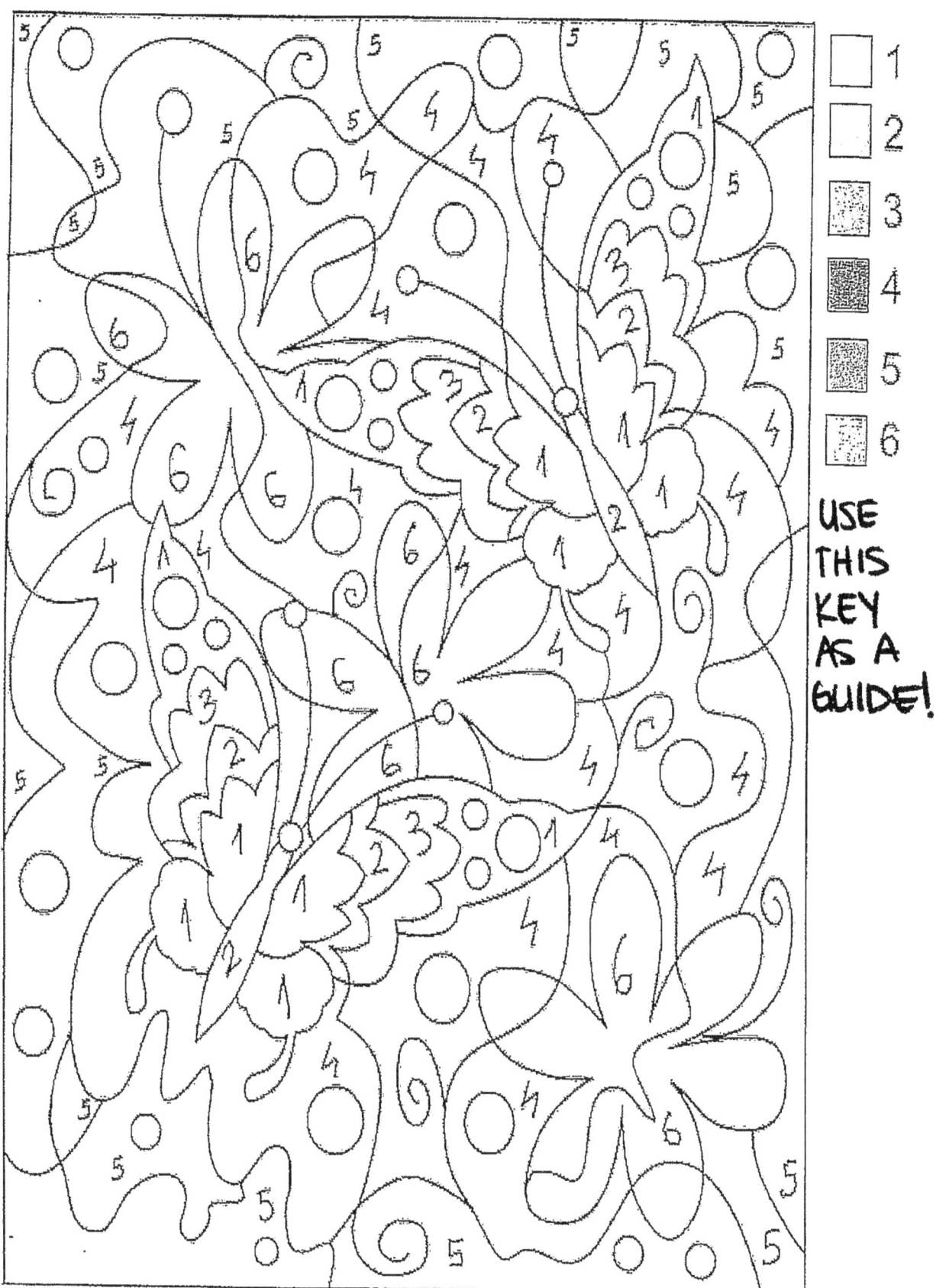

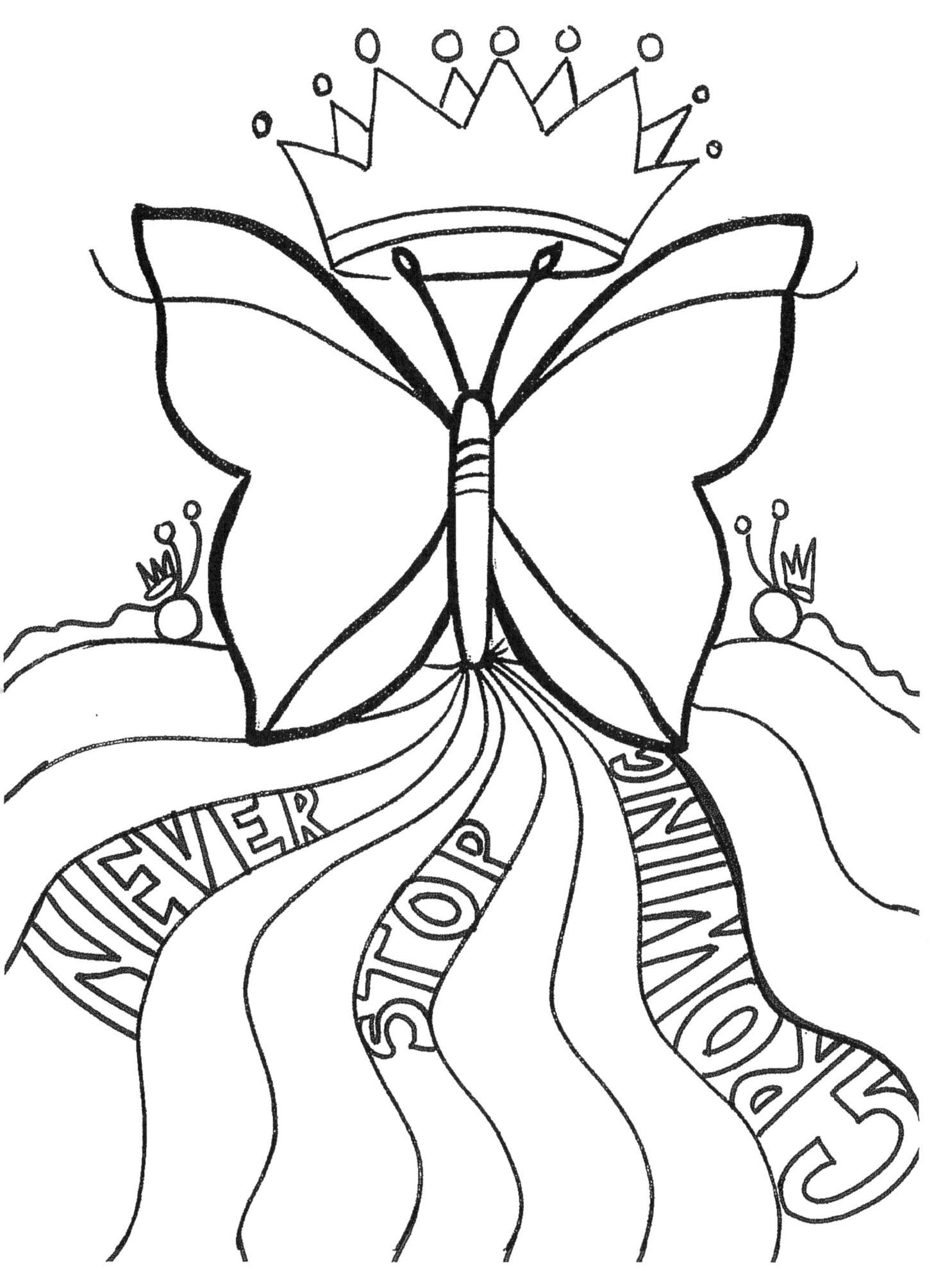

WHATS THE WEATHER?

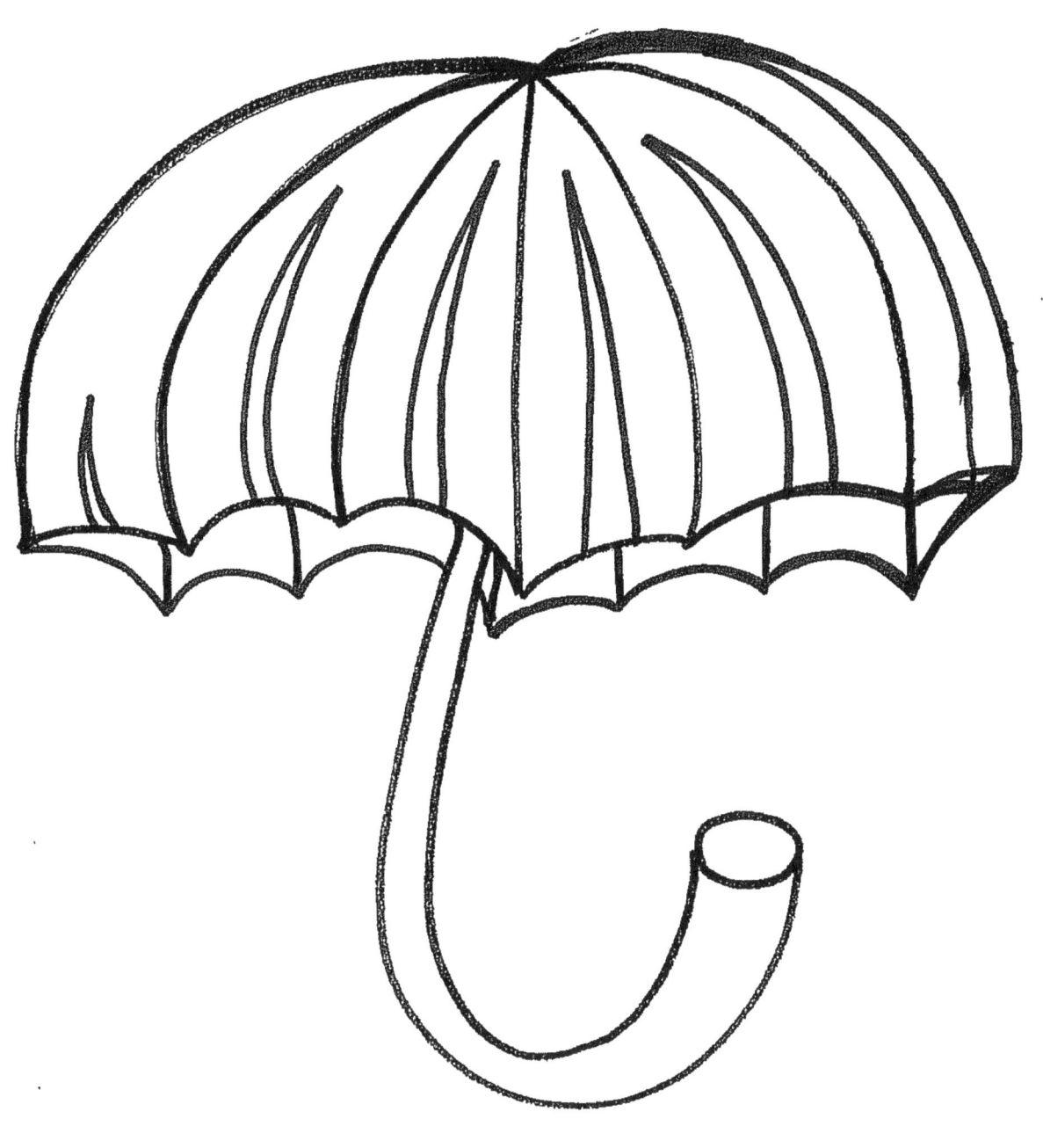

DRAW IN YOUR WEATHER FORECAST!

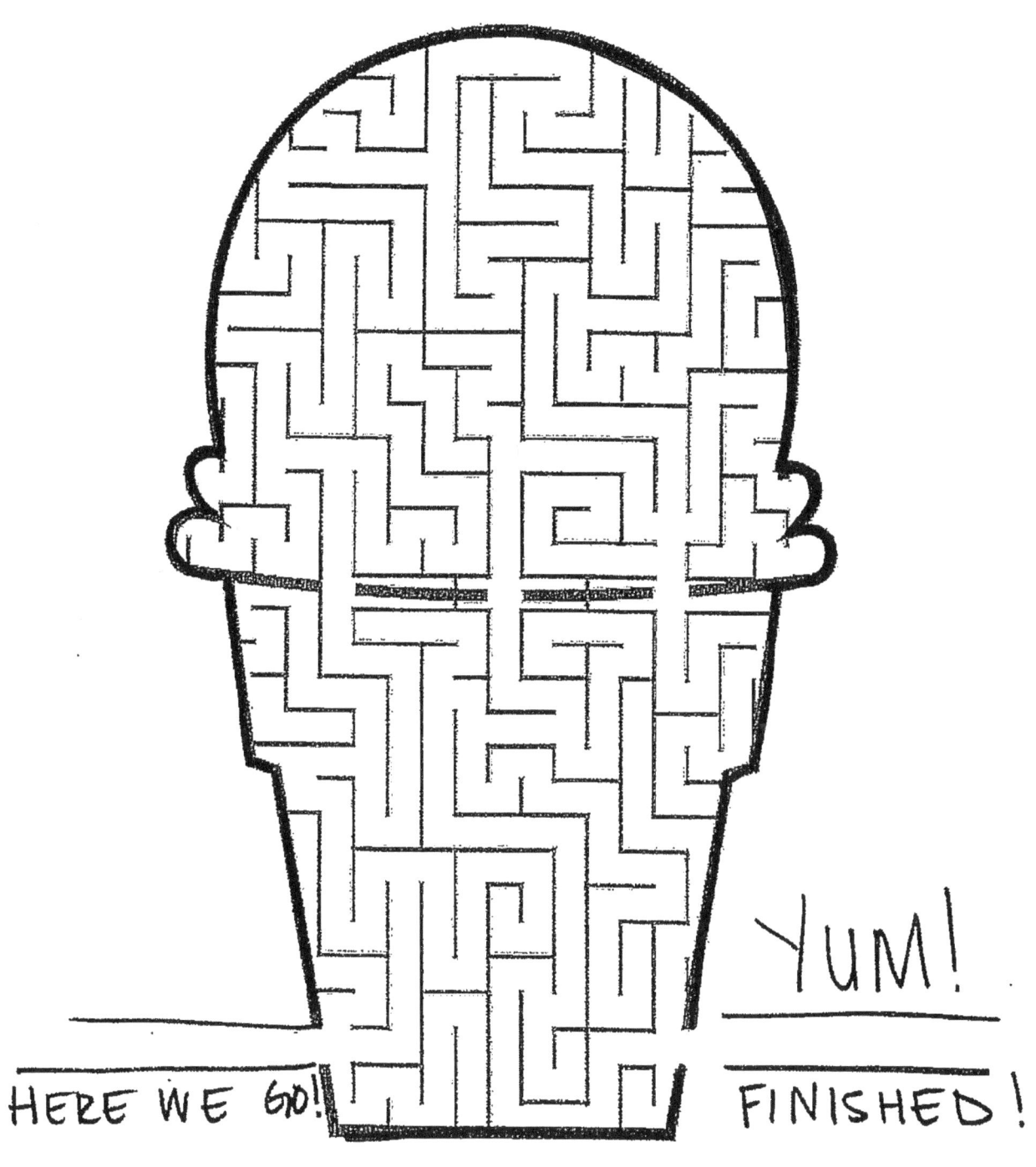

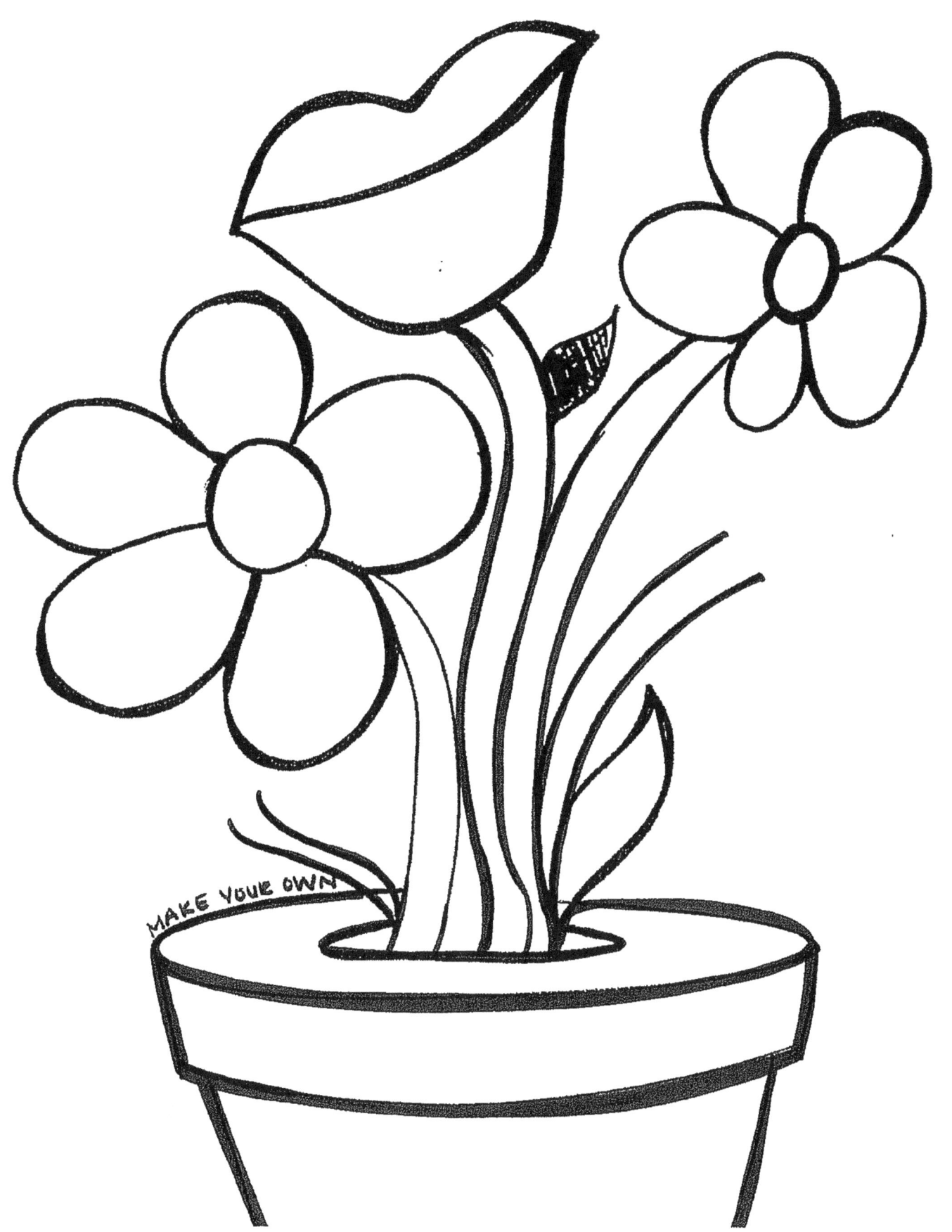

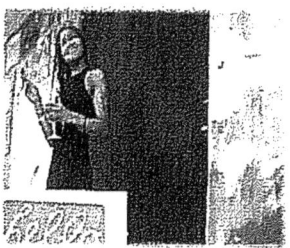 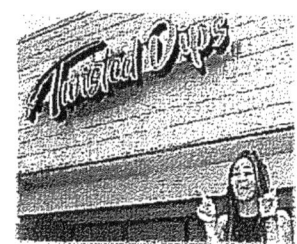 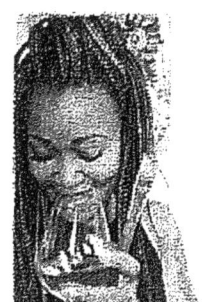

ABOUT THE AUTHOR

Kamille "Kam" Brown was born under the stars of August 26th as a Twin to her younger brother Andre. She is the 2nd of 4 children and the only girl. As a child, Kam fell in love with arts at an early age. She would draw, paint, sculpt and dabble in anything of the arts form. Throughout her younger years, she always wanted to be an entrepreneur. At such a young age, entrepreneur as just a big fancy word that not many of her classmates wanted to be. Fast forward to after high school, Kam married at a young 19 Years old. She then became a stay at home mom, while her husband worked. As her husband's birthday approached, Kam was intrigued from a bet placed by her Uncle of making a custom cake like the ones seen on TV! (At the time Charm City Cakes was MAJOR!) It was then, February 17th of 2011 that she created her first stunning ALL EDIBLE Custom Cake. From that day forward, her first business Kake By Design was born and she has been the artist behind hundreds of cakes! (She even did a cake for 2Chainz, Young Dolph ,Rick Ross and a few other celebrity clients!!) Although Kam had/ has great success as an Cake Artist, Kam thought it was time to do MORE! 2017 she decided to open Twisted Dips Art Studio! It was there that she continued to branch off and do more, such as one of THESE Great Coloring Books. There's no telling what she will think of next, but we know it will be great!

Make sure to check out Twisted Dips Art Studio!

(Where you can find Kam doing what she does!)

1395 Southlake Parkway

Suite A

Morrow, Ga 30260

Visit the website TwistedDipsATL.com for all upcoming and MORE

"Twisted Dips"!

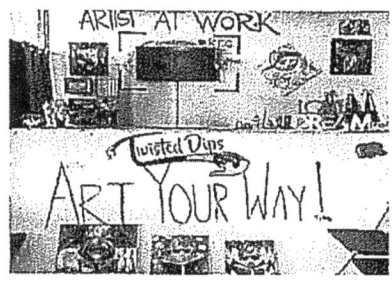

www.ingramcontent.com/pod-product-compliance
Lightning Source LLC
Chambersburg PA
CBHW062345220526
45469CB00008B/2837